Move over, Wonder Woman, th[...]
From the creative genius of awa[...] humor writer Molly
Stevens comes Boomer on the Ledge™, the answer to every
aging boomer's prayers. Do you worry you're just one bad knee
away from "Help, I've fallen, and I can't get up"? Fear no more for
Boomer on the Ledge™ has got your back! Dispensing health tips
and wine recommendations with equal aplomb, this Boomer
heroine is one for the ages…and ages of 50+ never looked more
inviting—or hilarious—than through the eyes of Molly Stevens.

-- Lee Gaitan, awarding-winning author of the Amazon #1
bestseller My Pineapples Went to Houston.

Molly Stevens has brought fun back into being a boomer. Who
needs an elf when we can have our own Boomer on the Ledge™?
This lighthearted look at life as a Boomer and bringing back some
Christmas Magic, was a delight to read. We all need more smiles
and laughter in our life and Molly's book certainly gave that in
spades. Let's start a Boomer on the Ledge™' Christmas tradition!
But really, I want my own Boomer on the Ledge™ all year round.

-- Sue Loncaric, writer at Sizzling Toward 60 and Beyond, riding
the wave of midlife with positivity, fun and laughter.

For years, I've sought that one, perfect feel-good-Christmas-elf-
related-aging-boomer-with-issues-madcap-picture-book. Who
knew it was right there inside the creative brain of humorist Molly
Stevens? That's the first place I should have looked! Boomer on
the Ledge™ is a chuckle and a gem. And those two rarely travel
together.

-- Dave Jaffe, award-winning author of Sleeping between Giants:
Life, if you could call it that, with a terrier.

Boomer on the Ledge

Molly Stevens

All Photos by Molly Stevens

Published 2017 by HumorOutcasts Press
Printed in the United States of America

ISBN: 0-9994127-0-1
EAN-13: 978-0-9994127-0-1

Acknowledgements

It takes a village to birth a book and I would be remiss without thanking the villagers who helped me through the labor pains.

Thank you Donna Cavanagh, for saying 'yes' when I asked if Humoroutcasts Press and Shorehouse books (HOPress label) wanted to publish this baby. You believed in The Boomer on the Ledge™ from your first introduction. Your admonishment to 'breathe' and enjoy the process has gotten me through the highs and lows that go with forty-plus weeks of gestation.

A virtual high five goes to Ed Cavanagh whose formatting and technical skills transformed a rough draft into a polished creation.

A heap of boomer gratitude goes to Brenda DeRoche. You brought my vision of The Boomer on the Ledge™ to life with your amazing sewing and artistic skills. The doll is everything I had hoped she would be thanks to you.

Thank you to my Facebook support group, 'Blog, Share, Love,' because you counseled me to pursue this concept and gave me confidence to persevere.

To my readers, I thank you. You are the catalyst for all of my writing, because even though I've been known to do it, I don't like to laugh alone.

Dedication

To Patrick
There is no one I'd rather hang on a ledge with than you.

Too Old For an Elf?

It's the time of year when families with young children rummage through Christmas decorations and dust off Santa's magical helper, the elf who sits on the shelf. Such a sweet Christmas tradition, having a spy embedded in the home, helping Santa judge whose names get written on the naughty versus nice list.

I understand why that little Elf is attractive. What parent hasn't dreamed of having watchful eyes reining in the little dears for a whole month?

Who is watching us boomers?

When you reach boomer status, however, no one is watching you anymore, neither Santa nor his little elf. If you haven't landed in jail by now or gotten in trouble with the IRS, it's safe for Santa and his elves to stop monitoring your behavior.

Since we are past the age of believing in Santa and his elves anyway, where do we boomers find our Christmas magic?

Molly Stevens

Introducing: Boomer on the ledge

I wanted to make a rhyme, but when one of the options for boomer was tumor, I decided to abandon the pretense of becoming a poet and feel thankful I could put a complete sentence together.

Boomer on the Ledge™

Why is the boomer on a ledge?

What aging boomer hasn't felt like he or she was hanging on a ledge, vulnerable to uttering the phrase, "I've fallen, and I can't get up?" Hanging precariously between danger and adventure?

Molly Stevens

Daily surprises

Young children awaken each morning with a sense of wonder when they search for the elf posed by exhausted parents the night before. Likewise, I never knew when or where my tousled little doll would appear, but she never ceased to amaze me with her daily surprises.

For those caring for elderly parents and supporting children, this sandwich is for you.

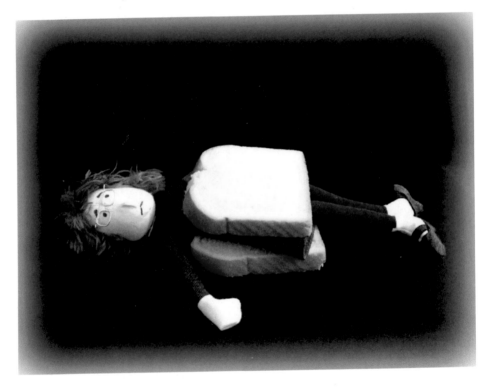

Boomer on the Ledge™

One day I came home from work exhausted and found this welcome sight.

Molly Stevens

When I couldn't find her, I abandoned my search to do some writing. She was there ahead of me with some great ideas.

Boomer on the Ledge™

I began to wonder if I was due for any health screenings when she reminded me it was time for my mammogram. Ouch!

Molly Stevens

She saved my life when she taught me the hazards of accessorizing.

Boomer on the Ledge™

Nearing the end of my career, she encouraged me to do some financial planning to alleviate my concern about money.

Molly Stevens

I smelled smoke and realized she was demonstrating my intolerance for uncomfortable clothing. There is nothing like roasting pantyhose on an open fire to get you in the mood for the holidays.

Boomer on the Ledge™

She called into question my belief that exercise is good for your health.

Molly Stevens

She made me laugh when I walked into the kitchen and saw her buried under Tupperware. Who hasn't had this nightmare?

Boomer on the Ledge™

She knows I am dependent on a hot cup of coffee to get me going in the morning.

Molly Stevens

I always eat a healthy breakfast, and I love it when she opens the cereal box for me. She does a much better job than I do.

Boomer on the Ledge™

Some days are tougher than others, and one day I found her drinking out of the dog dish. She thought it was gin.

Molly Stevens

The salt makes my legs swell, but she knows I still enjoy a good Lays.

Boomer on the Ledge™

One night when I couldn't sleep, I went to the kitchen for a snack. She awakened me to the danger of operating small appliances under the influence of insomnia.

Molly Stevens

One cold, dark December morning all I wanted to do was stay in bed with the covers over my head. Until she reminded me of the 'reason for the season.'

Where do you think you'd find your holiday Boomer on the Ledge™? Do you think she could help you rediscover your Christmas magic?

About The Author

Molly Stevens arrived late to the writing desk but is forever grateful her second act took this direction instead of karaoke or trampling competitors at the all-you-can-eat buffet. Molly believes humor is the emollient that soothes life's rough patches and promotes these convictions in her blog: Shallow Reflections. She won third place in the 2017 National Society of Newspaper Columnists writing contest and is a contributing author for These Summer Months: Stories from the Late Orphan Project, edited by Anne Born. She is a featured contributor for Humor Outcasts and part of the Bangor Daily News blogging network. Her guest posts have appeared on: Erma Bombeck Writer's Workshop, Better after 50, Sizzling Towards 60, Mostly Blogging, and Sixty and Me. Molly grew up on a potato farm in northern Maine, where she wore a snowsuit over both her Halloween costume and her Easter dress. She lives in eastern Maine, and when she's not writing, working or watching the New England Patriots win super bowls, she and her husband, Patrick, love to spend time with their son, daughter-in-law and two perfect grandsons. This is Molly's first book.

Made in the USA
Middletown, DE
22 October 2017